Triceratops

Written by Angela Sheehan
Illustrated by John Francis

Library of Congress Cataloging in Publication Data

Sheehan, Angela.
  Triceratops.

  Includes index.
  SUMMARY: Outlines the daily activities of a triceratops, a Cretaceous plant-eater whose hide and horns made it a fierce predator.
  1. Triceratops—Juvenile literature.
[1. Triceratops.   2. Dinosaurs]   I. Francis, John, 1942-   .   II. Title.
QE862.D5S46   1981   567.9'7   81-111
ISBN 0-86592-113-X   AACR1

Ray Rourke Publishing Company, Inc.,
Vero Beach, FL 32964

Brontosaurus
(Apatosaurus)

Pteranodon

Cetiosaurus

Dimetrodon

Iguanodon

Stegosaurus

Triceratops

Tyrannosaurus

Triceratops

Parasaurolophus

Ornithomimus

Ankylosaurus

A hairy animal, no bigger than a mouse, watched Triceratops as she kicked a blanket of sand over the three eggs she had just laid. The sand would keep them warm and well hidden while the young reptiles inside the shells grew big enough to hatch.

Laying her eggs and making them safe had been hard work for Triceratops. Now she was tired; too tired even to notice the little mammal or the other dinosaur that had sneaked up to watch her. The dinosaur, Ornithomimus, kept his thin body close behind a tree while Triceratops struggled clumsily over the rocks, looking for a place to rest before the sun grew too hot.

As soon as Triceratops had lumbered away, the little mammal scurried from its hiding place to nose for worms and beetles among the ferns. He was hungry. So too was Ornithomimus. And Ornithomimus liked nothing better than to eat the eggs of other dinosaurs.

Slyly, Ornithomimus picked his way to the nest and bent his long neck to brush the sand from his prize. The first shell broke with a crack, and the yolk spilled out. Ornithomimus licked up the sweet, warm liquid.

The egg tasted delicious. But it was the only one that Ornithomimus ate. For a frightful roar sounded behind him. No need to look, he took to his legs, leaping swiftly and nimbly over the rocks. Close behind him came the harsh sound of clawed feet, crashing and crunching over the ground. The monstrous Tyrannosaurus was bearing down on him. Only speed or slyness could save Ornithomimus now.

Triceratops knew nothing of the robbing of her nest, nor of the chase that followed. She rested in a

thicket of giant ferns as the sun rose high in the sky. Shaded by the broad green fronds, she drifted into a deep sleep. Some hours later, she was woken by the thud of heavy raindrops and the rumble of thunder. The rain beat down, drenching and flattening the ferns.

After the storm, the sun came out to dry the plants. Steam rose from the fronds and the smell of their freshness filled the air. Triceratops ate her first meal of the day. Slicing the greenery with her beak-like jaws, she munched her way through the thicket. Birds sang in the trees above her, small mammals scampered by her feet, and pterosaurs clung to the tree trunks.

Suddenly, there was silence. The birds ceased to sing, the mammals crept into their holes, the pterosaurs took to the air. Triceratops stood stock still. The only noise that could be heard was the sound of branches snapping beneath the heavy tread of Tyrannosaurus. All the animals waited in terror.

One dinosaur, Ankylosaurus, was standing directly in the brute's path. He sank to the ground and drew his legs in under his armor. Tyrannosaurus circled around and around him, roaring in fury. But Ankylosaurus was like a rock, too solid for tooth or claw to pierce, and too heavy to move. There was no way through his armor.

Tyrannosaurus had only one hope: to turn him over and attack his soft belly. Triceratops and the other animals watched from a safe distance as the great creature tried to heave him over. But no matter how hard he tried, Tyrannosaurus could not shift the stubborn stone.

Suddenly Tyrannosaurus gave up, and, in an instant, turned his anger on Triceratops. But instead of fleeing, she stood her ground, head down, as the great animal charged. Unable to stop in time, the savage creature screamed in pain as Triceratops thrust one of her great horns into his thigh. Now the mighty dinosaur could only limp away. The blood from his wound left a red trail in the ferns.

The other creatures in the wood were safe now. Tyrannosaurus would not bother them again until his wound had healed. Slowly the mammals crept from hiding and the birds began to sing and flutter in the trees. Triceratops plodded to the lake where she could drink and bathe. And, after some time, Ankylosaurus, too, was brave enough to push out his head and move carefully away. He looked about him as he went and swung his heavy tail from side to side.

The lake water was warm and silky. Triceratops wallowed in the shallows and bit the tasty tops of the horsetails that grew there. As the shadows began to lengthen, the insects stopped their buzzing in the magnolia flowers. And a chill wind began to blow. Triceratops clambered up the slippery bank, her feet squelching in the soft mud. Soon she must find a place to sleep.

As she left the lake, Triceratops heard the distant croaks of pterosaurs as they sought their nightly perches on the cliffs. She also heard a strange cracking noise that made her stop in her tracks. Peering through the twilight, she saw two Stegoceras dinosaurs charging towards each other. With a tremendous crash, their thick skulls clashed. Again and again they charged, while the rest of the herd looked on in silence.

Soon the battle was over. The weaker Stegoceras reeled backwards, unhurt, but unable to stand another attack. The other strode away, with his head held high and the rest of the herd following. As Triceratops went on her way, she passed the weaker one, trailing far behind his herd.

Now it was almost night and the wind blew colder. With no fur or feathers to keep her warm, Triceratops had to find a warm place to sleep. She headed for her favorite spot. It was a rocky hollow near where she had laid her eggs that morning. The rocks shielded her from the wind and a pile of dry ferns kept her warm and out of sight of any enemies. She could sleep safe and sound——until tomorrow.

Triceratops and the Cretaceous World

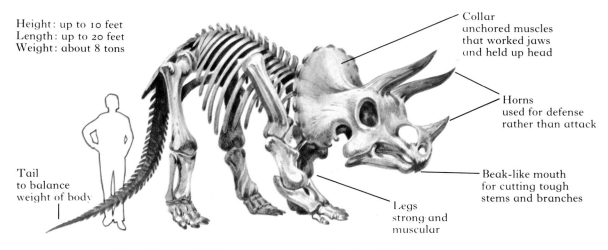

Height: up to 10 feet
Length: up to 20 feet
Weight: about 8 tons

Collar
anchored muscles
that worked jaws
and held up head

Horns
used for defense
rather than attack

Beak-like mouth
for cutting tough
stems and branches

Tail
to balance
weight of body

Legs
strong and
muscular

The skeleton of Triceratops compared in size with a man

When did Triceratops live?

Triceratops lived during the Mesozoic Era, or Age of Dinosaurs. The Mesozoic Era began 225 million years ago and lasted for about 160 million years. Scientists divide the era into three periods: the Triassic, Jurassic and Cretaceous. Triceratops lived during the last one, the Cretaceous.

What kind of dinosaur was Triceratops?

Triceratops belonged to a group of plant-eating dinosaurs called horned dinosaurs, or ceratopsians. The first ceratopsians were small creatures with little armor. But later ones like Triceratops were big and strong with dangerous horns and spikes. They were rather like reptilian rhinoceroses. The picture on the next page shows some of the different types.

Hot or Cold Blood?

The ceratopsians, like all the dinosaurs and many other prehistoric animals, were reptiles. The reptiles we know today, such as lizards and snakes, are cold-blooded creatures. They are as warm or as cold as the air around them. They cannot move about if the air is too cold. Birds and mammals are warm-blooded. They have fur, hair or feathers to keep them warm and their temperature does not change. They can live anywhere.

Many scientists now think that the dinosaurs may have been warm-blooded even though they were reptiles. They may have had hair and been able to move about much faster than modern reptiles can. But nobody knows for certain.

Reptiles and Their Young

In the story, Triceratops laid her eggs in a sand nest and then left them to hatch by themselves. Modern turtles and most other reptiles do the same. Scientists have found nests of fossilized eggs belonging to a ceratopsian dinosaur called Protoceratops. So it is most likely that Triceratops also laid eggs.

What did Triceratops eat?

We know how Triceratops ate from the shape of its teeth and jaws. It plucked or snapped off the branches of plants with its parrot-like beak. Then it sliced up the tough leaves and stems with its teeth. These had sharp edges and moved across each other like scissor blades. In fact, they were more like a meat-eater's teeth than a plant-eater's.

To move its huge jaws, Triceratops had long, strong muscles. The muscles were attached to the bony frill around its neck. The frill also helped Triceratops to hold up its enormous head, which reached 8 feet in length.

Plants of the Cretaceous

The plants that Triceratops ate and sheltered beneath were probably quite different from the ones we know today. A Cretaceous forest would have had lots of big ferns, conifers, palms, and plants called cycads (Ornithomimus is hiding behind a cycad on page 5). But there would not have been many of the trees with flowers and fruits that we see in our woods today.

Before the Cretaceous period there were almost no flowering plants at all. And even during the Cretaceous there were not many different kinds. One of the first flowering plants was the magnolia (see page 16). It was a long time before there was any grass. The ground must have been covered by moss or ferns.

Animals of the Cretaceous

Today the biggest and most important animals are mammals. But, during the Cretaceous, mammals were only the size of mice, almost too small for the mighty dinosaurs to notice. (You can see a mammal on page 5 and on several later pages.)

The fiercest of the dinosaurs were meat-eaters such as Tyrannosaurus (see page 9). Almost no creature was safe from its cruel teeth. Some animals, like Ornithomimus, could escape from it by running or hiding. Others had to rely on their strength or armor. Triceratops was only just tough enough to withstand an attack; a weaker animal, either older or younger, would probably have been killed. Ankylosaurus could fight off attackers with its big clubbed tail or sink down on its stomach and rely on its bony armor, as it did on page 12.

The oddest of all the animals in the story were the Stegoceras dinosaurs (see pages 18 & 19), sometimes called boneheads. Their skulls had as much as 10 inches of bone on them. They may have fought with other animals, or with each other over a female, perhaps, as deer do today. Their "crash helmets" would have stopped them bashing out each other's brains.

We know that there must have been many birds in the Cretaceous, although not many remains of them have been found. There were also great flying reptiles called pterosaurs (see page 11). They had light, leathery wings like bats, and could glide, though they could not fly like birds. They lived mostly on fish which they snatched from the water in their long beaks. Most of the other creatures in this book, crocodiles, insects and so on, have close relatives living today, so we know more about them.

Picture Index

Apart from Triceratops, these are some of the other animals that you can see in the book:

Things To Do

Try to think of animals living today that are like the dinosaurs in the story. Triceratops was like a rhinoceros. Can you think of a fierce meat-eater like Tyrannosaurus or a plant-eater with armor like Ankylosaurus?

Nobody has ever seen a living dinosaur, so we can only guess what they looked like from their skeletons. The artist who illustrated the story made Triceratops gray. You draw him the color you think he would have been, and try drawing the other animals a different color, too.

Make a model of a scene from the story using modeling clay for the ground and animals, and paper and card for the plants. You can make horns with sticks, armor with pebbles, and teeth with long-grain rice.

Some ceratopsian, or horned, dinosaurs

Protoceratops   Monoclonius   Styracosaurus   Triceratops